Book Desc

If you have hear_____encies, you may be wondering wh_____

Decentralized A_____ _____ — Are they really something new to the world? Are they legal? What's different about a DAO when compared to the Internet? After all, the Internet is decentralized. No one person or entity owns it, and it is autonomous in the way that it develops.

And the most important question — Why are DAOs important and relevant to you and your life as a citizen of today's world?

This book is designed to get the average Joe up to speed on how DAOs are creating waves in the technology and digital currency world and why you should know about this DISRUPTIVE technology. Just as cryptocurrencies have become common, DAOs are quickly becoming a more widespread concept.

In this book you will:

- Understand the fundamentals of DAOs and the technologies behind this concept of organizational structure
- Discover the benefits of this technology for you as an average person
- Learn how to make the most of this technology as it changes every industry around you
- Learn everything you need to know to be able to utilize this technology in several different capacities

The rate of change of technology is not slowing down, and our learning should not either. Click the Buy Now button and discover how DAOs are revolutionizing the world as we know it!

Decentralized Autonomous Organizations (DAO)

The Complete Beginner's Guide (Easy & Simple Introduction To The Organization Of The Future)

© **Copyright 2021 - All rights reserved.**

The content contained within this book may not be reproduced, duplicated, or transmitted without direct written permission from the author or the publisher.

Under no circumstances will any blame or legal responsibility be held against the publisher, or author, for any damages, reparation, or monetary loss due to the information contained within this book, either directly or indirectly.

Legal Notice:

This book is copyright protected. It is only for personal use. You cannot amend, distribute, sell, use, quote or paraphrase any part, or the content within this book, without the consent of the author or publisher.

Disclaimer Notice:

Please note the information contained within this document is for educational and entertainment purposes only. All effort has been executed to present accurate, up to date, reliable, complete information. No warranties of any kind are declared or implied. Readers acknowledge that the author is not engaging in the rendering of legal, financial, medical, or professional advice. The content within this book has been derived from various sources. Please consult a licensed professional before attempting any techniques outlined in this book.

By reading this document, the reader agrees that under no circumstances is the author responsible for any losses, direct or indirect, that are incurred as a result of the use of information contained within this document, including, but not limited to, errors, omissions, or inaccuracies.

Table of Contents

Decentralized Autonomous Organizations (DAO)

Introduction

Chapter 1: What Is DAO?
The Traditional Business Organization

The Structure of the Internet

Characteristics of DAOs

Chapter 2: Why DAO? Decentralized, Democratic Organizations
DAO for Business Owners and Investors

DAO for Customers

DAO for Stakeholders

Chapter 3: How Does DAO Work?
The Platform

The Smart Contract

The Operations

The Members

Chapter 4: The History of DAO
Wyoming DAO Framework

Chapter 5: Governance
Facets of Governance

Tools of Governance

Chapter 6: Pros and Cons of DAO
Advantages

Disadvantages

Notable Examples of Decentralized Autonomous Organizations

Chapter 7: Risks and Limitations

Chapter 8: DAO and Corporations

Humans, DAOs, and Corporations

DAOs and Company Performance

Vulnerabilities

Chapter 9: DAO and Decentralized Finance (DeFi)

Chapter 10: 7 Leading DAOs in the Crypto Space

Chapter 11: Five Bold Predictions about the Future of DAO

Chapter 12: The Future of DAO – Institutions of the Future

Conclusion

References

Introduction

The cryptocurrency space and technology, in general, are expanding at a rate that we have never witnessed ever before in history. Amidst these changes, we have experienced a pandemic, causing the entire world to go into a state of lockdown. This is an incredibly challenging time for people worldwide, but in some other respects, this was a time of extreme growth and development.

Blockchain technology has been around for over a decade now, but it has really gained traction and caught the attention of the masses in the past two years. Most people only see the rise in the value of cryptocurrencies and the increase in the number of digital currencies available today. They fail to see all the activity that is happening in the background, which is making it possible for these technologies to come to the forefront. Blockchain is not only changing the game for digital currencies and giving fiat currencies a run for their money, but it has also given rise to the technology behind DAO, Decentralized Autonomous Organizations. It is this technology that is revolutionizing business and organizational structure as we know it.

While digital currencies are only changing the way we look at money, the way we work with monetary institutions, and how we invest, DAO is changing institutions of all kinds at an organizational level.

You may think that it doesn't make any difference to you who the CEO is in a leading multinational, but if you understood the kind of change that is possible simply because of a change in the organizational structure of entities, you might well reconsider your stance.

DAO is a technology that is not only limited to businesses. In reality, given the abilities of this technology, it could change the way you pay your bills, the way you look at education, and it could change the way you vote. In fact, it could change the government that you vote for.

As a management solution, this technology may give us a better way to run human society as a whole, rather than just parts of it.

However, it is just as complex as it is revolutionary. To give you a solid understanding of what this technology is, where it is coming from, and where it is heading, this book is going to briefly delve into the most important aspects of DAO and explain how it relates to your life.

Chapter 1: What Is DAO?

As the name suggests, these are decentralized organizations with the autonomy to make decisions independently based on information they gather on their own.

Companies using the DAO structure are predominantly found in the digital world, specifically in the cryptocurrency industry. However, to better understand this concept in context, it would be helpful to look at the traditional structure of organizations and the Internet and contrast this with decentralized autonomous organizations.

The Traditional Business Organization

If you look at the business model for any business in any industry, there is always a hierarchy - management, stakeholders, and a single person or group of people who are given the responsibility to make decisions. In both small businesses and large multinational corporations, power is highest at the top and slowly decreases as you move down the hierarchy.

The Structure of the Internet

The global network has gone through a few different stages of evolution since its inception in the early '90s. The purpose of the Internet was to be a platform where people from all over the world would be able to come together to connect, share ideas, and be part of a global village. It is designed to be a system with no single owner, with no single decision-maker, and a system that adapts itself to the requirements of users. In a way, you could say that the Internet was the first entity that demonstrated some of the traits which characterize the modern decentralized autonomous organization. However, things didn't go exactly according to plan, and taking a look at some of the major milestones in the development of the Internet will help to highlight this fact.

Web1 - This was the Internet right after it was launched. It was a brand new technology running on brand new technology, and few people knew anything about the technology or the hardware that it operated on. Computers had been around for a while at this point in time, but the Internet was new. The Internet consisted mainly of small websites, personal web pages, and some business websites and allowed users to access information through directories. Many of the businesses that would later become major players in the IT world were still very small endeavors being managed by single-member teams or very small teams. There was only a limited amount of media available online at this stage, and the Internet was in a highly autonomous phase with no one to govern its behavior and performance.

Web2 – Technology prices dropped significantly, high-speed Internet became more affordable and possible, and the Internet experienced a massive influx of users. With improvements in technology and the lower prices at which hardware and software were available, many people started looking at computer engineering as the new golden profession. This was when the Internet experienced much change, in terms of what it provided and how it performed.

However, the Internet was now also home to some massive corporations such as social media platforms and large high-traffic websites like popular search engines. These large companies were having a massive impact on how the Internet performed and was to quite an extent influencing the behavior and growth of this global network.

Web3 – The Internet entered a phase where it was not only accessible through personal computers but was also gaining a lot of traffic from a variety of smart devices. Growth is still incredibly high, and the things that are possible through the Internet are increasing exponentially. More complex services are offered through the Internet, and more advanced technology such as AI makes this shift possible. However, the Internet giants are getting larger in size, and with this increase in use, their influence is growing.

Characteristics of DAOs

If you notice, businesses and the Internet up until its third evolution have relied extensively on human input, whether that is in the form of decision making, data gathering, content generation, or simply day-to-day functionality.

As a decentralized autonomous organization, a business or an institution significantly reduces its reliance on human input. Using complex smart contracts, DAOs are now able to do everything independently. This includes doing some extremely complex things, such as running large corporations or managing solutions for a human-run business.

To bring a DAO into perspective, you can better understand it by looking at its unique characteristics.

1. **Free For All** – Anyone has the right to freely enter and exit the DAO given that they meet eligibility criteria. There is a set of rules and a set of basic requirements that every member must abide by and adhere to. Anyone who does can join. There is no limit to how many or how few members a DAO can have. It is open to all.

2. **Equality** – Whether you are a new member or a founding member, there is equality in terms of what members can and cannot do. Moreover, the input that they provide in terms of suggestions is also equally important to the DAO regardless of who provides it. No one is anyone's boss. Rather, everyone works together for the greater good.
3. **Maintenance-Free** – The DAO doesn't need any assistance from humans specifically to carry out its duties. Once it is set into motion, it becomes a self-sustaining entity able to perform without any human input.
4. **Transparent** – Everything about the company is clearly documented. Even the Smart Contract, in essence the ideology and strategy upon which the organization is founded, is completely transparent for anyone to view.
5. **Cheap And Scalable** – Given the way these companies run, they have very low operational and maintenance costs. Moreover, their simple design is easy to scale.
6. **Based On Blockchain** – At the back-end of every DAO system is a blockchain. The blockchain platform may change, but essentially these systems can only exist on a blockchain ecosystem.
7. **Secure** – The fact that they are based on a blockchain, they are digital, everyone has access to all resources, and every change in the organization is traceable makes these organizations extremely secure.

These are the fundamental elements of a DAO which are present in the organization regardless of the kind of work that the business performs. Through such an organizational design, we can use DAOs to create businesses, perform certain tasks, govern other entities, and even to be independent systems that work together toward a bigger cause. The possibilities for DAOs are limitless.

Chapter 2: Why DAO? Decentralized, Democratic Organizations

Every institute and organization impacts society at large. The intensity of the impact it has varies depending on how large or small the organization is and the value of the work that it provides. Overall, while the organization impacts the people it employs and the people it directly caters to through its products or services, it also affects various stakeholders that may not be directly connected to the organization.

As DAO companies exist predominantly in the digital arena and are closely associated with crypto, essentially, they can have a global effect. With the number of people interacting on the Internet growing daily, the impact of these companies is on the rise. The structure of DAOs is such that it makes it very easy to have a big network and to be able to cater to a large audience without having to do much in terms of structure. This ease of expandability is one of the things which makes DAOs unique in their performance. These unique abilities also make the DAO organizational structure attractive for businesses in a wide variety of industries. In the near future, we are likely to see this concept grow into many new industries and be adopted by different businesses, at least partially, if not as an entire replacement to their existing structure.

We can understand the significance of DAOs from the perspective of business owners and investors, customers, and broader society as stakeholders.

DAO for Business Owners and Investors

This type of organizational structure is a dream for any business owner or investor. It gives them complete control over how the business is set up, what it's aimed to do, and how it is going to achieve those goals. More importantly, it eliminates the need to manage people and removes the possibility of human error. More than just human error, it completely eliminates all the problems that business owners and investors face when they need to deal with human teams and, in effect, even eliminates the need for an HR department. It's an organization that will not have varying trends. It is self-learning and requires minimal input or attention.

Apart from the obvious advantages to its performance, this is also a style of company that can be extremely profitable if the product, the market, and the workflow can be properly mapped out in advance. There are very few variable costs and operating expenses in an organization that relies on computers to carry out its tasks.

DAO for Customers

Customers benefit from these low costs because they can acquire goods and services at reduced prices. If you look at any business in the world right now that caters to even a small audience, the majority of its expenses are salaries paid to staff or rent for physical and digital assets. Should the company shift toward becoming an autonomous digital organization, the many benefits it will receive will be passed on to clients in the form of competitive prices, better stability, more consistent products, and even improved quality.

Moreover, their input may be far more valuable to a DAO than it is to a traditional company since the DAO will process the information without any prejudice or predisposition. This means customers will find it much easier to have a DAO company incorporate their demands or feedback and provide them with products and services that consider that input.

DAO for Stakeholders

Bigger businesses are better businesses for society. It's easy to see how beneficial businesses are for an economy and a society when we look at the numerous examples of businesses that are exploiting the environments within which they operate. Even though these businesses are harming the environment, countries are still happy to accommodate these large companies since they provide many other benefits. In some cases, even though the benefits outweigh the costs, one of the biggest problems is that these large companies are not completely transparent about how they conduct their business. The people involved in and affected by these organizations don't know how much harm the companies may be causing.

This is not going to be the case with DAO businesses. Like machines, these businesses only do what they are designed to do, and anyone can see their objectives and design. All changes that take place are through the consensus of the majority, and big decisions do not rest in the hands of a handful of top executives.

All these factors contribute toward making DAO-style businesses a great addition to society as they benefit every part of that society. However, as crypto gains momentum, DAOs will also play a big hand in bringing digital currency to the forefront.

Chapter 3: How Does DAO Work?

Though the concept of a DAO is relatively easy to understand, the way these organizations can do these amazing things is a bit more complex. From a technical standpoint, there is a lot of technology and digital expertise that creates a fully functional DAO that can do everything necessary to become a successful business.

In terms of how DAOs actually work, there are a few key areas that we can look at to understand this better.

The Platform

Essentially, everything that happens in a DAO is in the form of a transaction. For this reason, all decentralized autonomous organizations are based on and backed by a blockchain. Most commonly, DAOs are developed on the Ethereum blockchain. When DAOs select a certain blockchain as their platform, they are designed using the tools available on that blockchain, and they use the tokens of that blockchain as 'shares' for members. On Ethereum, the language used to 'write' these DAOs is Solidity. However, the tokens serve more than just being considered as shares. They represent the token holder. Therefore, similar to shares, the majority token holder has the most influence on the DAO.

The Smart Contract

After the platform on which the DAO is based, the second most important thing is the Smart Contract. This digital document is the heart and soul of the organization. Everything in terms of how the company will operate, what rules and regulations it will adhere to, how it will make certain decisions, and even what the physical outlay of its digital infrastructure is going to be, are all part of the smart contract.

This is the document that will either make or break the decentralized autonomous organization.

The smart contract is made prior to the launch of the organization. This is what developers and investors will be working on before launch and will continue to work on after launch. However, after the company is operational, making changes to the smart contract is possible, but it will depend on a number of variables. Moreover, every change that is made to the contract is recorded, just like every transaction that happens. Please note, transactions are not only cash movements. Everything that happens in a DAO is known as a transaction. Whether that is a change of rules or the addition of a new member, all movements or changes are recorded.

The Operations

The DAO performs exactly like a regular, human-run corporation of its kind. As a basic example, if the DAO is an e-commerce store, it will buy products, list them on the website, create invoices, manage payments, send out deliveries and create account statements at the end of the month.

Over the course of time, it will change how it does things to improve performance. It will look for new suppliers, and it will market itself and work toward expansion and growth.

The only difference is, there isn't a human or group of people doing all these things. It's all code provided by the smart contract.

Changes that happen, for instance, if the DAO decides to add a new product, can be based on member votes. If the DAO has ten members, and seven of them agree that a certain new product should be added, it will be added. The changes that occur are based on majority consensus. Without the consensus of the members or those members that hold the majority of the tokens, changes can't be pushed through.

The Members

To be a member of a DAO, you will offer the company investment in the form of the tokens you buy, or you may be a developer and can offer your skills.

However, each DAO will have its own unique criteria for letting people join, and anyone who meets those requirements can join. There is no limit on the size of a DAO, and unless a maximum membership is set, it's free for all.

Being a member of a DAO is very similar to being a shareholder in a company. You will benefit from its gains both in terms of profits and the increase in your token value in the company, and you will be able to influence company decisions proportional to the voting rights you have.

Should he DAO not be a business entity but a governing body or an institution of any other kind, it will operate in exactly the same way as a human-run version of that enterprise does. The only difference is it will be digital. It will still retain all of these components, and they will still function in the usual manner.

Chapter 4: The History of DAO

Decentralized autonomous organizations have been a part of the business organization literature and organization theory for several decades. Experts such as Beckhard, Freeland, and Baker have been discussing this organizational structure for decades. However, it was not until recently that real-life examples of everyday companies using this model came into existence.

With the onset of the Internet and virtually based enterprises, we saw the first wave of organizations that could generally be classified as DAO systems. These were decentralized systems that had some level of autonomy. These pioneering systems were known as Decentralized Autonomous Corporations (DACs), though this name was only given to them later on after cryptocurrencies had started to appear. People who were part of the digital currency culture referred to these older systems as DACs and how they were similar to the DAO framework that cryptocurrencies aim to achieve.

However, even though DACs did share a lot of the performance characteristics and organizational structure with modern DAOs, the main difference lay in their application. Companies following the DAC protocol were large companies that needed an alternative to the regular stock exchange solution that existed for public companies. In this manner, these companies were more about corporate governance than they were about giving technology the center stage and allowing it to function as a free entity. The shift from using technology simply to manage a company's activities to using technology to create autonomous companies was the big change seen with the introduction of DAOs.

Even with this viewpoint, we can still see how restricted the idea is when we consider the many limitations that modern DAO systems have, even when used with blockchain platforms. However, it was still a big shift toward truly decentralized autonomous organizations, and it was a blockchain that made this possible. It's important to note that there was no involvement of a blockchain in the DAC systems, which is why their ecosystems were very different from those of blockchain-based DAOs.

On one end, some argue that cryptocurrencies themselves are DAOs, while on the other end, there are those who say only companies that employ smart contracts and exist on a blockchain network can be categorized as DAOs. However, at the core of this debate, the concept of the DAO remains the same. What varies is what people classify as a 'correct' implementation of the system and how this defines the terms "decentralized" and "autonomous."

In May 2016, the Ethereum based system known as The DAO was the first DAO to gain popularity and attention. It exemplified how a decentralized autonomous organization could exist, but that organization fell apart after a digital attack in June 2016.

Even though this pilot project wasn't an incredible success, it was an incredible learning experience for users and developers of DAO systems. Since then, the DAO system has grown exponentially, and there are a number of functional DAOs today. These blockchain-based organizations are doing everything from raising funds for charities, allowing people to transact products and services, being a source of investment, and performing many other functions. The most important thing is that it allows people to collaborate directly with each other without the need for an intermediary.

As cryptocurrencies are expanding, people are slowly starting to understand the potential and feasibility of DAOs. Some countries are taking proactive steps to make DAOs a part of their future.

Wyoming DAO Framework

In March 2021, lawmakers in Wyoming voted to pass a bill that would allow DAOs to be registered as legal entities in the state. The bill came into action on July 1, 2021. Soon after this bill came into action, the first US registered DAO came into being named American CryptoFed.

Under this law, DAO-based companies would enjoy all the rights that traditional limited liability companies (LLC) enjoyed. It would have legal protection, it would be a part of the tax system, and the company would be able to do anything that a human-run organization of the same nature would be allowed to do.

Wyoming became the first state to legalize DAO-based companies, and this goes to show how much support there is for this type of business in the state. However, Wyoming has always been at the forefront of business development and has always taken the first step when it comes to evolving and expanding its economic interface.

Chapter 5: Governance

Governance is a bit of a complex and a debated matter when it comes to DAOs. As these organizations are decentralized and autonomous, it requires a lot of work for them to be governed smoothly to qualify as being democratic and representative of the population. Moreover, the way in which and the effectiveness with which a DAO is governed has a big impact on its legal status, in the trust that is gained with its human audience, and even in the way that it can be applied to various industries.

While these organizations aim to be decentralized, they can only be decentralized in terms of their architecture and how their physical components exist in the world. Architectural decentralization allows different people or groups of people to run independent nodes and master nodes in some cases however they please as long as it supports the network. In terms of geography, these nodes can be located anywhere in the world, although this will depend on which countries and regions allow them to exist within their jurisdiction legally. However, the protocol will always remain the same for all nodes and all actors. Essentially, the system is still working according to one plan. Therefore, it cannot be decentralized in terms of its aims and objectives.

Facets of Governance

DAOs are meant to be democratic systems, but how this democracy is exercised depends on two distinct and prominent factors. Firstly, the DAO is dependent on a flat hierarchy that lies within the organization and constitutes its various members that play the role of decision-makers, investors, and developers of the system. |Second are the external governance tools, like nodes and servers on which the DAO is based and the blockchain upon which it exists.

For both of these facets of governance, there is a lot to consider. There is a lot that can be compromised, and even though it does potentially offer a lot of flexibility and efficiency, it may be hard to achieve these goals.

Tools of Governance

Every DAO system depends on a few tools to make good governance possible.

Identification – As a first step, the smart contract that constitutes the essence of the DAO needs to be identified and acknowledged. Based on this document both the DAO and the people involved in it will make decisions. This is the foundation of the governance protocols in the DAO.

Enforcement – This is the process through which the system is able to implement the rules outlined in the smart contract and the fact that these rules and regulations govern all actors.

Tokens – This is the process through which the DAO is given value, the medium through which people can receive any monetary gain from this system. The blockchain the token is based on plays a big role in this process, and this will have a big impact on the effectiveness of the DAO itself.

Infrastructure – This includes everything tangible required to keep the DAO alive and include everything that goes into making the formation of the DAO possible. Everything from developers to end-servers plays a role in the infrastructure.

Transparency – This is one of the pillars of the DAO framework as it gives every actor just as much access to information as any other actor. This transparent nature of the platform makes it reliable - though the reliability of this depends on the developers and how well they can give members a clear image of what the business can do.

Trust – Transparency is great, but on its own, it does not verify the other person to a given actor. Therefore, systems need to be 'taught' how they can bring people together and make it possible for them to transact by using the DAO as a verifier without the need for a third party to service the deal.

However, in terms of business operations, the kind of governance system that a DAO adopts depends entirely on its applications. For instance, business DAOs that are taking the form of LLCs will need to have an internal structure that is correct for that kind of business. On the other hand, businesses that are looking to be DAO-based real estate management companies or people who are simply looking for a way to safely send and receive funds will need a governance system that meets the requirements of that field of work. There is no one-size-fits-all rule about governance, but all DAOs in all industries will use some basic building blocks.

Chapter 6: Pros and Cons of DAO

When considering the decentralized autonomous organization, where there is a range of advantages, there are also limitations. Overall, the DAO is aimed to improve many of the limitations that we face with traditional businesses, but it does present us with another unique set of challenges. For some businesses, the DAO will be more of an effective strategy than for others. In certain fields of work, the use of DAO may not be relevant at all, where the business depends entirely on the human touch or presence.

Decentralized autonomous organizations have been one of the most ambitious projects in the cryptocurrency space to date. Yet despite their interesting premise, DAOs are still very much works-in-progress experiments. We will expound on the pros and cons of decentralized autonomous organizations and review some of the most notable projects that have been or are proposing to hold a DAO ICO.

Advantages

One of the biggest advantages of DAOs is that they are based on open-source code that is freely available for anyone to modify. People worldwide collaborate on mediums such as GitHub to develop the code for these digital companies. This means that the entrepreneurs behind the company don't have to spend a lot of money on development, and they get input from a wide range of very talented people. This opens the doors for a lot of brainstorming and makes it possible for the project to grow and develop into something much more comprehensive. Moreover, with such a large and diverse group of people working on the project, the whole task can be completed much sooner and much more efficiently.

Just like in the development phase, once launched, these businesses have a global reach. Investors and developers alike worldwide can come together to be a part of the business created. Regardless of whether the company operates internationally or not, the people behind the company can easily participate from wherever they are in the world.

While the applications of decentralized and autonomous organizations are limited at the moment, they have the potential to revolutionize several industries. Many of the industries that could significantly take advantage of the DAO structure are already in the digital currency space but face difficulties, such as decentralized finance (DeFi) service providers.

Acting as a central authority that is reliable and one that has a wide reach, DAO systems can help bridge the gap between people who are willing to interact with other individuals across the world but want a platform that they can trust. Systems that use DAO are highly reliable as they are based on extremely secure Bitcoin platforms and offer security far greater than any other kind of organizational structure. Moreover, combined with the fact that these systems can only see fundamental structural changes when the majority votes it in, this is not something that happens every day. They offer a very long-lasting and consistent platform through which people can interact.

This safe community, combined with the fact that it is a safe platform through which people can exchange currencies, makes it perfect for facilitating business and any other activity that requires money to change hands.

The idea of a DAO is very simple: it is a contract that takes the form of a computer program capable of automatically executing the terms of its contract. Put differently; a DAO is a computer program that mimics the functions of a board of directors or an executive management team. And instead of using company resources to achieve its goals, it uses capital contributed by shareholders in the form of cryptocurrency. Here are some of the advantages of decentralized autonomous organization:

1. No Single Point of Failure

One of the most significant advantages of a DAO is that it is not susceptible to human error. This is because the blockchain-based smart contract code is immutable and will forever remain on the blockchain unless the code is re-written. In addition, a DAO does not have any single point of failure since it runs on a decentralized network that employs multiple nodes.

This means that even if one node fails, the whole DAO will not collapse. For example, the hacking of The DAO in 2016 left it compromised and led to the theft of 3.6 million Ether coins. Yet despite this major setback, the Ethereum ecosystem continued to function as normal.

2. Transparency

Since a contract is a code that runs on a blockchain network, it runs autonomously. This means that the company's operations are fully transparent and visible to all shareholders. Furthermore, the DAO will not incur any management fees since it does not employ a team of managers and executives.

The only transactions that will be executed are those that have been specifically authorized by shareholders. This eliminates the need for any third-party service providers. To elaborate with an example, if a company spends $50 million to purchase five machines for its factory, the fees will be much lower than if it had employed technicians and workers to manufacture the machines.

3. Low Overhead Costs

Since the blockchain is a decentralized technology, most of the costs associated with running a DAO are distributed along with the blockchain network. For example, unlike most businesses that employ an IT team or pay for the maintenance and upkeep of their technological equipment, a DAO does not have these costs. It does not even have a physical location since it only exists in cyberspace. The only cost remaining is that of employees who will directly contribute to the company's goals.

4. Democratic Decision-Making Processes

In a DAO, decisions are taken by shareholders who vote via a smart contract code, so each shareholder has a voice in managing the company. In addition, they control how profits are distributed and can authorize a DAO to initiate a crowdfunding campaign. Unlike most companies, though, shareholders have no say in how their money is being used and have no right to conduct audits of its management.

5. Favorable Conditions for Startups

DAOs can be used by startups to raise capital without needing a physical entity and all the red tape involved. The DAO can also be used to incentivize developers and entrepreneurs into contributing to its codebase or growing its community in exchange for DAO tokens. Since a blockchain-based DAO is not susceptible to outside influence, it can operate independently of the government and serve the interests of its shareholders without having to contend with regulations.

Disadvantages

A serious concern for people looking to incorporate DAO as a structure and even for developers of these systems is the intense conflict of interest. With so many people participating in the organization, it's only natural for there to be a conflict in interests. When this arises, the only way to resolve it is through majority votes, and if one person or a small group of people have the majority of the tokens, essentially, the power of decision-making is once again skewed.

Secondly, as this is an extremely valuable digital platform with many forms of DAOs being valued in hundreds of millions of dollars, it is prone to security problems. Cybercrime is on the rise every day, and as digital currencies and digital organizations become the norm, cybercriminals are also shifting their attention from traditional companies to these modern entities. This means that companies employing the DAO structure may be looking at spending vast sums of money on security.

Also, as these companies make use of a very flat hierarchical structure, decision-making can be a very slow process. Moreover, as even the most basic decisions need the entire population of members to vote a decision, it can mean that changes happen very slowly. While for small companies, this may not be a big problem, as companies grow and the number of decisions that need to be taken increases, it can result in extremely slow growth as so many things are in the pipeline to be decided upon.

Despite their interesting premise, decentralized autonomous organizations still have a lot of legal obstacles to overcome. This section will highlight some of the most notable disadvantages of DAOs and how they can be resolved in the future.

1. Unregulated

Currently, DAO's offer potential shareholders a great degree of operational transparency. However, they are still in their early developmental stages and have yet to be integrated into the legal system; this means they are not yet considered a legitimate form of business organization, which, in turn, means it's not favorable to use them to establish a startup. In addition, many nations have yet to develop a legal framework to regulate them. It's clear, therefore, that a DAO will not be a viable form of business in these countries.

2. No Physical Office

As mentioned earlier, a DAO does not have a physical office since it exists virtually. This means it does not have any real employees, which leaves the company itself without a legal entity. In addition, it cannot be taxed since part of its services are offered for free. While this can be seen as a benefit since it relieves the company of financial obligations, its shareholders cannot sue the DAO for losses. To do this, they must first establish an agreement with the DAO to form a separate physical entity.

3. Legal Uncertainty

The lack of legal certainty regarding DAOs usually revolves around their existence only in cyberspace and have no physical form. However, it can also be due to their decentralized nature. Furthermore, the ambiguities surrounding the concept of "smart contracts" and the legal requirements to form a DAO make it even more difficult for governments to regulate. For the time being, decentralized autonomous organizations should proceed with caution, as their operations are technically illegal in most countries.

4. Lack of Credibility

Since DAOs currently exist only in the virtual world, there is no way for anyone to verify their credibility, and they can be used to facilitate criminal activity. This problem is not insurmountable since the technology is still new, and issues like this will surely be resolved in time. Moreover, most organizations that use blockchain-based technologies are fully transparent, so it should be easy to determine if they are legitimate.

5. No Corporate Org Chart

Since a decentralized autonomous organization is not required to have any employees, it cannot be managed by a corporate organizational chart. Public companies are required to have a detailed org chart to assist shareholders when voting on key issues. Since decentralized autonomous organizations do not have employees and cannot hold votes, they cannot be effectively managed. This is where DAO tokens come in as they offer shareholders a degree of control over the entity.

Notable Examples of Decentralized Autonomous Organizations

There are a few notable examples of decentralized autonomous organizations that have attempted to solve some of the legal and logistical issues outlined above. They include:

1. Dash

This entity is the foremost decentralized autonomous organization to focus on privacy and governance. Dash has a dedicated DAO that is managed and funded by the blockchain and its users. A proposal is submitted to the network, which then decides if it will be funded. It's a democratic governing body that uses a voting system to resolve disputes and reach a consensus. With a strong track record that spans many years, Dash has been able to fund some of the biggest projects in the cryptocurrency space.

2. DigixDAO

It's a decentralized autonomous organization that focuses on disrupting the gold industry by tokenizing physical assets using the Ethereum blockchain. DigixDAO uses smart contracts to manage its operations and voting processes. The DAO is supported by DGX tokens, which are used to reward those who vote on proposals. There's a strong correlation between the success of DigixDAO and that of Ethereum. Both have grown exponentially over the last two years and have a strong community.

3. Aragon

This is an organization working to build a digital jurisdiction. It's currently in its fundraising stage and has already raised over $30 million worth of Bitcoins. Since it operates as a DAO, it's managed by the blockchain and its users. All of Aragon's investors are also entitled to vote on proposals that will impact the growth of the organization. By relying on a consensus-based model, decentralized autonomous organizations are experimenting with new governance models that could one day lead to greater transparency and accountability.

4. BOScoin

A decentralized autonomous organization, BOScoin focuses on democratic decision-making through the use of smart contracts. It's different from what most decentralized autonomous organizations are trying to do since it concentrates on providing financial services to the unbanked. BOScoin's DAO focuses on providing financial services to low-income families in developing countries. It's an ambitious goal that currently only the blockchain is capable of tackling. With democratic decision-making processes, BOScoin can keep its stakeholders informed of the progress it's making towards achieving this goal.

5. First Blood

First Blood uses a decentralized autonomous organization to manage its eSports platform. The power of First Blood's DAO lies in the way it incentivizes good behavior. Those who are penalized by its smart contracts will have their tokens taken away. Those who are rewarded will have their tokens locked up for future use. First Blood is one of the first decentralized autonomous organizations to focus on solving social issues. Its DAO is built around the expectation that people will act in their best interest.

Currently, decentralized autonomous organizations have not been adopted on a massive scale, so it's still hard to say what the implications of this kind of structure will be for organizations in certain industries. However, what is clear is that they are not free of problems and will need some development to overcome these difficulties.

Chapter 7: Risks and Limitations

While there are different disadvantages and potential problems that people need to be aware of before they get involved with a decentralized autonomous organization, there are a few inherent risks to this design of an organization. Moreover, while DAOs aim to take a big step forward in terms of the evolution of organizational structures, they aren't without their risks or limitations.

First, let's consider the performance risks of DAOs. Blockchain is an extremely powerful and extremely technical form of technology. One of the main reasons it is such a capital-intensive process to mine coins and generate blockchains is the intense computational power required to do just that. To give you an understanding of just how much power this is, to run the network that powers Bitcoin, one of the pioneers and leading cryptocurrencies on the market today, the Bitcoin ecosystem uses more electricity than over 150 countries of the world combined. While this is an incredible amount of resources to power a single network, it indicates how much processing power is required to keep these systems alive.

Similarly, with DAOs being based on these blockchain technologies and cryptocurrencies, running a decentralized autonomous organization is not a simple or cheap job. More than just the power requirements, the amount of technical expertise that is required to get this technology off the ground is incredible. Then the operational expertise is another matter. Even though these systems are designed to grow on their own and carry their own weight, at one point or another, human intervention will be required to perform duties that are not covered by the smart contract. Moreover, there are going to be times when human intervention is necessary to manage unforeseen circumstances.

On the same lines, the fact that this technology requires complex hardware and software to exist, not everyone will be able to become a node or really participate in this endeavor. This is a technology that will be limited to people who have the resource to make it possible, while the general population will still be able to reap the benefits of its existence as consumers of its products or services.

One of the most well-known decentralized autonomous organizations was known as 'The DAO.' It was a pioneer of this form of technology and did achieve a good level of success though it was a single cyber-attack that brought it down. This attack in June 2017 cost The DAO several million Ether Tokens which had an estimated market value of over $50 million at that time. After this attack, not only did The DAO take a hit in its reputation, but the Ether network at large also saw a fall in consumer trust and consequently token prices.

This attack on the DAO was made possible by exploiting the organizations' code, which goes to show that the reliability and security of such organizations depend heavily on the competence of the developers.

This leads us to the risk of developing such endeavors through crowd-sourced development programs. After all, what is being built is going to potentially be a multi-million dollar system that will be home to the data and assets of millions of people from across the world. Is it really wise to put such responsibility on a large group of developers that have no relationship to each other and are not bound by any formal boundary? They are all inputting what they think is good, and while their intentions may be sincere, can it guarantee that the final product is optimal?

On the topic of exploitation, it is important to note that it is not only the central DAO system that is at risk. Since all its peripheral operations are also digital, essentially, it relies on a web of digital services to operate, and any of these services could be compromised. Rather than exploiting the central network itself, which may be heavily guarded, exploiters always have the option to attack the broader web within which it exists.

Finally, as is the case with any technology, we can't be entirely sure of the risks and limitations of the DAO systems until they are used and applied to the real world. While other technologies that are significantly cheaper and less complex to use are easily tested, the same is not the case with DAO. The only way to iron out problems in any system is to put it to use and then troubleshoot as problems come up. With a system as complex, large, and as sensitive as a DAO, this is a risky and expensive proposition.

Chapter 8: DAO and Corporations

DAO systems are all about corporations and revolutionizing the way they operate. While the features and technologies of DAO will have a big impact on the overall structure, design, and performance of an institution, the main change is going to be the organizational structure and the fact that it will no longer require humans. At least, humans won't be necessary for the internal operations of the organization.

One of the important things to note is that DAOs will not be limited to businesses. Any form of corporation that aligns itself with the DAO structure can adopt this technology and gain benefits, whether that is a social platform, a business, a political party, or even a government. Considering the nature of DAO, it's safe to say there are several industries in which it simply isn't possible for businesses to take up the DAO system. Even if they chose to, it wouldn't be a financially viable option. On the other hand, several organizations are in perfect condition to accept this technology, and it goes without saying that they would benefit immensely from it.

Humans, DAOs, and Corporations

DAOs have built up a reputation for themselves and are widely regarded as organizations that will not need humans, causing many people much distress and having them worrying about unemployment again just as they have recovered from the stress of employment problems caused by the pandemic.

Overall, this is true. Nearly every process that a business or an organization performs on a daily basis can be coded into the smart contract and then delegated to computers to manage. However, there is still a need for humans in various stages of the DAO.

At the very initial stage, humans are needed to develop a smart contract that accurately reflects the activities of that organization. Moreover, security protocols and best practices also need to be developed by humans for the DAO to execute.

But more importantly, DAOs are evolving systems that are democratic and take the consensus of the majority to make a decision, and this **is** a majority of humans. For every change made to the smart contract and every decision made by the DAO, it will rely on human consensus, a consensus of most token owners.

Moreover, the involvement of humans in the blockchain and the DAO give it value that attracts other entities to work with it, and that attracts other humans to become part of the network.

DAOs definitely will reduce the burden on humans, and the DAO will now perform many things that humans did, but they won't entirely wipe out the need for humans.

DAOs and Company Performance

Performance, costs, and profits are the main attractions for businesses that are looking to adopt DAO. On the other hand, social organizations see the transparency of the system and the ideal environment for democracy as the most attractive features of the system. The features of this system appeal to a wide range of organizations which is why we are likely to see it being adopted by more than just businesses. In fact, many of the currently available platforms that are employing DAO systems illustrate what a diverse range of services can be generated through this organizational style.

Ranging from e-commerce stores to crypto developer groups to DeFi service providers, DAOs are helping out in many ways. Moreover, the fact that these companies are valued in the hundreds of millions of dollars shows us just how valuable this technology is and how much people are willing to invest in it.

Vulnerabilities

Even by digitizing their organization through DAOs, businesses still face their fair share of security vulnerabilities. This was best demonstrated in the attack on The DAO in 2016, just a month after its launch. The culprit turned out to be a loophole in the smart contract.

This goes to show that while digital technologies do present us with a lot of functionality, they are still prone to problems, and it will take a while before the DAO structure can be refined to meet modern standards. Moreover, the only way to understand the potential risks of such systems is to use them in the real world and apply them to various industries. Only through real-world testing can we understand their dynamics and the kind of difficulties they may face when working in certain applications.

Chapter 9: DAO and Decentralized Finance (DeFi)

As of now, the DeFi space is the primary industry in which the concept DAOs are being applied and used. There is potential for DAOs to be used in a wider variety of businesses and industries. However, even within the Decentralized Finance sector, it is yet to be widely adopted and implemented. Even with the dozens of cryptocurrencies currently listed on exchanges around the world, only a handful of those actively using the DAO structure for their operations.

It can be argued that cryptocurrencies are almost DAO systems on their own. As such, DeFis that employ various cryptocurrencies are, in fact, DAO businesses. This may seem to be an appropriate classification at a surface level, though it fails to hold true upon closer inspection.

One of the main differences between cryptocurrencies and a purely DAO-based system is that digital currencies still rely on human involvement and human interaction to generate any kind of value. Moreover, there are a few stages in which the digital currency relies on human input to move it forward.

When the digital currency is being developed and mined at the very first stage, it is entirely human dependent. The whole process of writing out the cryptocurrency code in the language of the native blockchain is done by humans. Just like human developers produce a smart contract for the DAO, the blockchain behind the cryptocurrency also requires human input. Secondly, the mathematical calculations done by mining rigs to generate the cryptocurrency tokens are done by computers, but this entire process is made possible thanks to human input. The cryptocurrency cannot mine its own tokens and requires a lot of human input to get the ball rolling.

Now, while the digital currency's initial construction is human dependent, it doesn't get any less dependent on humans even after the initial stages. It takes humans to invest in the currency for it to gain any value at all. In fact, the main reason why Bitcoin prices stayed so stagnant for so long was simply because people weren't willing to invest their money in something new and so radical. Slowly but surely, as people started working with Bitcoin and the Bitcoin blockchain was deployed to other applications, people saw value in it, people started to trust it, and consequently, prices started to rise. This holds true for any cryptocurrency and any technology, for that matter. Until people start using it, the masses will not adopt it, and the technology will not gain value.

Defi services and cryptocurrencies, in general, are used for a few different tasks. Most commonly, crypto is becoming a source of investment; people buy coins and wait for them to rise in value. Those living in regions where digital currencies are being used to transact products and services use this money just as they would otherwise use fiat currency. They pay, they lend, and they purchase using crypto. Moreover, those who create applications using the blockchains behind these digital currencies use these tokens to pay for their work and the resources they use.

While all of these things are excellent, the problem remains that these are all things that humans are doing through the DeFi services, and they aren't things that the DAO is doing on its own. If it were a pure DAO, there would be no human interaction. The system would in no way be dependent on humans to exist, but if tomorrow humans suddenly stop using cryptocurrencies altogether, these DAO systems would serve no purpose.

However, this is an idea that can be applied to any DAO. After all, organizations are meant to serve a purpose, and they exist because there is some function they provide to humans.

It's also important to note that even in a pure DAO system, and even with cryptocurrencies and services in the DeFi industry, the fact that they are both dependent on majority consensus to reach a verdict for any decision does, to some extent, take away from their autonomous nature.

Whether it is a DeFi system or a DAO-based organization in a different industry, it will always have a dependence on human input, especially in the case of decision making.

Chapter 10: 7 Leading DAOs in the Crypto Space

After the fall of The DAO in 2016, people were shaken, and the DAO technology did take a hit, but it was not long before people were demanding more DAO solutions, and developers took the step forward to provide them with what they wanted. Today we have a number of DAO systems that are performing a variety of tasks. Among this small group of companies, there are a few that stand out ahead of the rest.

In the crypto space, there are many blockchain-based projects built on the basis of the decentralized autonomous organizations' concepts. In a nutshell, a DAO concept implies that no single entity is in charge, but rather all involved parties contribute to the running and decision-making process. Such an organization can run independently from human interference, thanks to smart contracts, while providing safety through network decentralization. Now, the question is: what are the leading DAOs in the crypto space? Here's a list of seven projects which have achieved significance and look promising for the future.

1. MakerDAO

This platform brings together the Dai Stablecoin and Ethereum to create a system that protects people from highly volatile cryptocurrencies. It allows users to create their own stable tokens that can exist within a certain price range and can live relatively stable priced lives as the environment is designed to regulate this price. Token Maker can also be used as a recapitalization resource and is serving this function well. It is an active platform that has regular voting. One of the smart things about this platform is that there is a time difference between voting and the implementation of the change to prevent any financial corruption.

MakerDAO stands for Maker Decentralized Autonomous Organization and is an initiative created through a collaboration of different professionals in the fintech sector. At its core, MakerDAO is a blockchain platform on which anyone can issue and manage their token. The most essential part of the MakerDAO system is a cryptocurrency known as Dai. The value of one Dai equals one US dollar, which, as well as being a unique selling point, allows for cryptocurrency to be used in the real world. It also ensures stability since one Dai always has the same value of $1.

The MakerDAO system uses a product called Collateralized Debt Positions (CDP). It works by opening a position using collateral in the form of Ethereum (ETH), and after paying a stability fee, users are given Dai. MakerDAO stands out due to its versatility since it not only allows users to generate their tokens but can also be used by businesses. MakerDAO is seen as a platform that will facilitate the running of DAOs and decentralized applications (DApps) in the future. With a strong team and their token, Dai, MakerDAO is a project to look out for.

2. DAOstack

With the rise of DApps, developers need a place where they can come together to work, and that is exactly what DAOstack aims to do. It serves as a global community for people to develop any kind of application or service that they would like to collaborate on. Moreover, if you are a developer and you see another project that you would like to be a part of, you can do that on DAOstack. It is a unique platform that has a unique use for tokens as well.

DAOstack, or simply stack, is a platform that provides the tools and infrastructure needed for starting and running decentralized autonomous organizations (DAOs). Stack is often referred to as an operating system for collective intelligence since it provides the necessary tools for implementing collective decision-making processes. DAOs are organizations that have no single leader but are managed by all members, who will collectively vote on issues. There are many benefits to running a DAO, which is why stack is a decentralized solution to many of the problems experienced by organizations.

For example, stack provides a versatile and user-friendly framework for implementing DAOs. The smart contracts used by stack enable the implementation of complex governance models without sacrificing the quality of interactions. Another positive aspect is stack being open-source. This type of framework is free to download and use, and it can be modified by anyone, making it an innovative solution for running DAOs. By providing a viable and safe platform for DAOs, DAOstack is one of the leading DAOs in the crypto space.

3. **Digix**

Digix is a household name among those that trade precious metals as this serves as a specialized marketplace that caters to gold trading. This ecosystem consists of two tokens. One is the DGX (Digix Gold Tokens), in which each token equal's one gram of gold. The other is DGD (Digix DAO Tokens); this is the token that voters use to voice their concerns. While DGC is completely backed by real gold, DGD values depend on the performance of the platform.

DigixDAO stands for Digix Decentralized Autonomous Organization and is a project built on Ethereum (ETH). It has a two-token system that is composed of a stablecoin known as DGX and a token that gives its owners governance power in the form of votes. There are two use cases for DGX. The first is to make payments in the real world, while the second is the long-term storage of value. Regarding voting and governance, DigixDAO relies on the PoS (Proof-of-Stake) protocol to allow token holders to make decisions. To run a vote, token holders must deposit their tokens, and voting ends when the majority of users have deposited their tokens.

The deposits that are put into the vote determine the number of votes. Users with more tokens in their possession have more voting power and, therefore, can make decisions for the benefit of the whole network. The collateral for DGX tokens is audited by third-party organizations to make sure there are enough assets in reserve to support the price of one DGX, stabilizing its value stable and making it reliable. By being a DAO built on Ethereum, DigixDAO is a project which consists of a strong team and has many benefits.

4. IMMO

This DAO platform hasn't been launched yet, but its interesting and unique characteristics ensure its inclusion in the list. According to High1000, a well-reputed decentralized cryptocurrency community, this DAO will be based on 'valuable resources.' Moreover, High1000 is playing a big part in developing this platform and will play an active role in the platform once it's launched. More importantly, the High1000 will also be a guarantor to investors of their rights, which speaks volumes about this community's trust in this platform. This is definitely a DAO to keep an eye out for.

IMMO is a project that promises to combine all existing cryptocurrencies into one global network. At the same time,

IMMO functions as an autonomous mechanism for the creation of cryptocurrencies tied to real-world assets. To make this happen, IMMO has its blockchain fueled by a stablecoin called UTILITY that is pegged to one ounce of gold. This stablecoin has many benefits since it's far more stable than most cryptocurrencies, making it an excellent store of value.

UTILITY will also be used to transfer funds between different blockchains, allowing users to easily manage transfers. Another benefit is IMMO being a decentralized platform that allows anyone to create their cryptocurrency. In other words, all real-world assets could be represented by IMMO and its UTILITY stablecoin, which is a huge benefit for the finance and blockchain worlds. Having a strong team and many benefits, IMMO is one of the most promising DAOs in the cryptocurrency space.

5. Aragon

This is an interesting organization as it is a DAO itself; it facilitates others to develop their own DAOs through its services and its platform. The company claims that it has helped bring over 1000 DAOs to life and says the combined value of these DAOs is over $300 million. While token holders of this platform can vote for changes on the platform, they also can partake in any projects that are being built using this platform—a treat for DAO investors.

Aragon is a DAO that provides an easy-to-use interface for launching decentralized organizations. It offers many benefits, including the ability to create and run decentralized organizations. Other benefits include voting on issues, handling the funding of an organization, and using different DApps within one platform. The Aragon Network is a platform built on Ethereum that is specifically designed for DAO creation. It's important to mention the Aragon Network doesn't use any tokens of its own. Instead, it's fueled by ANT tokens that are used for governance and to pay for transactions on the network.

By being open-source, Aragon is free to download and use. The platform is entirely governed by the community that supports it. It has no central authority overseeing the network. It puts users in control of their data and voting power, allowing them to make decisions to benefit the network. Aragon is one of the leading DAOs in the crypto space because of its many benefits and because it is free to use. The project has a strong team with many years of experience in the finance and blockchain world. This is one of the most promising DAOs in cryptocurrency and has a bright future.

6. GnosisDAO

Based on the Gnosis platform, this DAO aims to help developers working on DeFi applications. The GnosisDAO looks at various market forecasts and studies the requirements of each market to provide its hosts with highly optimized, in-depth information. While this is a relatively new DAO, it is gaining a lot of popularity for the services that it offers.

Gnosis (GNO) is a prediction market platform built on Ethereum. This project offers several benefits, including decentralized financial tools and an easy-to-use platform. The goal of Gnosis is to make financial tools accessible to anyone with a smartphone. As an Ethereum-based platform, Gnosis has its own native GNO token that can be used to make predictions. Users are required to pay a small fee before making a prediction, which can be paid in GNO. Users are also required to hold GNO to have their predictions accepted. This ensures they put time and effort into making successful predictions, which is good for the system as a whole.

By predicting the outcome of events correctly, users receive rewards. They also have the opportunity to make big profits if their predictions are correct. The platform offers a variety of tools that are easy to access, including an open prediction market and aggregator. Gnosis can be used as a way to make bets on sports, elections, and other high-risk betting markets. It's one of the leading DAOs in the crypto space and offers many benefits and opportunities to users. By being open-source and fueling the network with its native token, Gnosis is one of the most promising DAOs of 2021.

7. MetaFactory

This DAO is a large-scale consumer-oriented business selling everything from jeans to shirts to caps. While retailing apparel is one aspect, the main aim of this platform is to crowd-fund various clothing and even allow mainstream clothing manufacturers to benefit from the crowd-funding that it can generate. It is a modern take on the traditional manufacturing process and allows users to benefit from not only token price but also in the form of profits when they invest in new ventures through the platform.

MetaFactory is a DAO designed to help make the funding of retail product manufacturing easier. It's an open-source platform built on Ethereum, which makes it decentralized. The platform offers many benefits, including increased transparency, efficiency, and the ability to create customizable products. One of the main benefits of being on the MetaFactory platform is that it offers an easy-to-use interface. For example, users can create templates that can be used to manufacture customizable products.

As a decentralized platform, MetaFactory offers many benefits for both companies and customers. For example, it helps to significantly increase the output and quality of products. From a company perspective, it creates better management for production and inventory. Customers benefit from more customizable products and faster delivery. And, like other DAOs, being decentralized also reduces costs. For example, all transactions are publicly recorded on the blockchain, which helps reduce fraud and is done without any central authority.

MetaFactory is one of the top DAOs in the crypto space. Whether you are a company or a customer, MetaFactory has many benefits, and its platform is easy to use. The project has already established itself as one of the leading platforms for making customizable products, which will only grow in popularity in the future. It's open-source and is fueled by its native token, which is used for all transactions on the platform.

There are several DAOs in the crypto space, but each one offers something different. By doing a reasonable amount of research into each entity's pros and cons, you will be able to make an informed decision as to which one best suits your needs. Some DAOs are open-source, while others use a native token to power transactions. Many of the top DAOs are open-source and have a large community supporting them. MakerDAO, Aragon, and Gnosis are some of the leading DAOs in the crypto space. They offer many benefits and use their native tokens to fuel transactions. MetaFactory is another decentralized autonomous organization that has established itself as one of the top options for making customizable products. The beauty of DAOs is that they will continue to develop and grow with time.

This diverse range of DAOs goes to show how widespread this market really is. Whether you are a developer, an investor, or looking to take on the management of a DAO server, there are many options for you to choose from.

Chapter 11: Five Bold Predictions about the Future of DAO

The fact that blockchain and DAO systems are likely to grow and gain a lot more traction is not only represented by the number of projects going on and the amount of money each of these projects is able to secure but rather by consumer behavior. All of this activity in the blockchain space is in direct response to consumer demand; developers and investors alike are not only spending themselves on these projects out of passion but because they can see a market for it in the future, and it is a big market.

Moreover, as DAO systems grow increasingly efficient and streamlined, it is more than likely that this technology will spill over into other areas in which it can be used.

Here are a few things that seem extremely likely considering current consumer behavior and the trajectory of DAO-based trends at the moment.

1. Corporate Governance through DAO

Traditional governance systems are extremely inefficient when compared to the governance capabilities offered by the DAO system, as well as being more expensive and less flexible. Today, we can see many companies moving toward blockchain technologies to improve and automate several areas of their business, and it seems quite possible that they will soon move towards optimizing the biggest asset they have, human management. A digital solution to governance is far more resilient, it's more adaptable, and it offers all of its benefits at much lower prices. For businesses, it is a more profitable proposition in every sense.

2. DAO Systems Infiltrating Traditional Governments

There are hundreds of companies in the world that are currently managing revenues and budgets that are more than several countries in the world. In fact, some of the top companies in the world have more revenue and more money to manage than several nations combined. While governments are meant to voice the concerns of their population more than just managing the financial resources of a country, a system that can implement democracy more effectively and be a better money manager will be better at both these tasks. When people see how effective DAO systems are in business and in the management of other service-based institutions, they would definitely want to see those improvements in their governments as well.

3. Global Blockchain Government

Today we have several institutions that serve as decentralized and autonomous global guardians. They assist states in any way that they might need assistance, but the way they operate, the way they are funded, and the impact that they have on nations that they assist are very close to what the behavior of a DAO is, with the exception that they rely on a human workforce. Considering the infinite growth potential of a DAO system, its ability to scale up to meet challenges of any size, it makes sense to have one global government or at least one global platform to assist countries and those in need, rather than having multiple institutions. The only major difference will be that this global government will be digital and will be more efficient than any human-run enterprise of that size could be.

4. Investment and Accounting through Blockchain

One of the biggest advantages of DAO-based systems is their financial prowess. Being computers and software at their core, they are extremely powerful in financial calculations, forecasts, and estimations. There is no doubt that these DAO-based systems will have a big impact on the financial sector even outside of the DeFi space. It will only take a little fine-tuning to get these systems to expertly manage anything related to finance for large and small applications alike.

5. Blockchain in Utility

DAO systems combined with blockchain platforms offer an unparalleled level of management power. This will be exceptionally useful when organizing businesses with very large pools of consumers, such as utility companies, postal services, and even e-commerce platforms. These businesses see millions of daily transactions and the best way to optimize performance is a digital system that is self-sufficient. Even for human governments and private sector businesses, DAO systems and blockchain solutions can be very profitable in these areas.

However, as time goes on and these services get more streamlined for specific tasks, we will better judge where and how these systems will expand. Even given their current state, it is clear that their application will be widespread, and most likely, extremely beneficial.

Chapter 12: The Future of DAO – Institutions of the Future

The recent Covid-19 problem has highlighted the limitations of our traditional business models and also highlighted the benefit of digital systems and the Internet. While the Internet was experiencing a high level of growth prior to the pandemic, that one event put technology into fifth gear and turbocharged the rate of digital change globally.

In a way, we were forced to decentralize everything. Schools, businesses, tourism, food, every single industry took the impact of the pandemic. In each of those industries, the businesses that could sustain themselves and even recover were those that could incorporate digital systems and decentralize their networks. They were able to carry out their businesses remotely. This required a high level of autonomy, and it required them to make use of digital systems they never intended to.

Now, even after that, we are back from the pandemic, and things in most parts of the world are going back to being somewhat normal. But businesses are extremely unlikely to go back to their traditional ways, not only because there is always the imminent threat of another wave of the virus, but because they have tasted the benefits of technology. Many businesses not only survived the pandemic, but they also thrived, and after the lockdowns lifted, they continued to use their new style of operations and are experiencing better efficiency, less stress, and higher profits. What's not to like about it?

If we add DAO systems to this situation beef-up performance with blockchain solutions, there is no doubt that these businesses and institutions would have benefitted even more.

If basic features like team collaboration software, remote working services, and digital marketing could be this effective, there is no reason for DAOs not to be even better. It's also important to note that many of the services that businesses and institutions have relied on during the pandemic are services that they opted to choose haphazardly, and they were the best solutions they could find at that moment in time. If they could have invested the time to really research and find optimal services for their applications, then the results would have been even better.

Just before the pandemic, cryptocurrencies were taking a hit. They had been stagnant for quite a while, and things weren't looking like they were going to improve anytime soon. However, during the time of the pandemic and just after, things started to improve in early 2021. Companies that had only held a few thousand dollars' worth of assets were now owners of millions of dollars. It was a time when the crypto space saw a radical influx of people, causing prices to skyrocket, and now that these new investors have seen such a high percentage of growth, it is unlikely they will be stepping down anytime soon.

More importantly, this influx of investment in cryptocurrencies also meant that these platforms could spend more in the direction of project development, and we also saw a big rise in the number of DAO projects being undertaken. With such keen interest from investors and so much funding available, these projects launched very quickly, and now we find ourselves in a marketplace with a plethora of very young DAO systems. Considering the amount of work that has been put into these systems and the financial backing that they have secured, it is quite likely that we will see good things coming from these. However, just as no one had anticipated the pandemic, it's hard to judge which direction things will go in, though everyone is hoping for the best.

At the very least, DAO has proven to be extremely effective management software for companies. Companies that are using these systems are by no measure small garage companies. They are multi-million and even multi-billion dollar firms that have a lot at stake.

DAOs provide such a robust and multi-talented platform for stakeholders that it is hard to say no to this option. Things that would otherwise have taken a lot of money and would have required stakeholders to go through much red tape can very easily and quickly be sorted out through DAOs and blockchain.

With companies adopting these technologies rapidly, even if they don't entirely transition to them, they will definitely play an integral part in the structure of these organizations in the future.

Conclusion

Some would argue that the DAO system and the blockchain technologies haven't yet matured enough, and they still need to be tested to be considered usable for the average person. Others will argue that they have proven their worth, and now it is up to us to use them the right way to harness their true potential.

The recent uptrend in cryptocurrencies and DAO systems has sparked individual consumers' interest, as they can be part of this huge market, and large companies interested in getting ahead of the competition by getting their hands on the latest and the greatest.

The good news is that the slump that we had seen in these technologies in the past decade has now become completely overcome thanks to the interest of millions of active users in this space. Things that in the past seemed like they would take forever to come to the mainstream have now nearly made it completely to the mainstream and the major markets and industries worldwide.

Not only are consumers and developers of these technologies very willing and active in bringing them forward, but even various governments and institutions around the world are taking steps into making them a reality. The fact that DAOs are gaining legality is an extremely promising development and will naturally lead to more countries and regions following this course of action. This vets DAOs as reliable forms of technology and will help by leaps and bounds to attract more people toward these platforms. One of the biggest limitations that cryptocurrencies, blockchains, and DAOs were facing in the past was a lack of trust. These are expensive technologies, and their high investment requirements make them very risky.

Now with legal backing and the fact that they are being used in so many ways, people have a lot more avenues that they can take.

With so much momentum behind these technologies, it is not difficult to see them making more progress in the next two years than they have made in the past ten years combined.

Moreover, as we develop new uses for these technologies and are applied to more industries, institutions other than businesses will likely be looking forward to trying out these technologies if not formally implement them in their organizations. With the right management and correct development, there are very few areas, if any at all, that cannot benefit from DAOs and blockchain solutions.

In the past year, the value of the cryptocurrency market and the asset value of DAOs has gone from being in the thousands to the billions, and in the next few years, it could climb even higher.

If this is the case, then just five years from now, we could see the whole world making legal amendments to accommodate these technologies and revolutionize the way countries are governed.

At the end of the day, everyone wants to profit. Whether that is in the form of money or a better environment that they live in or even a more streamlined life that is possible due to DAOs and technology, the purpose is to grow. These technologies are clearly helping us achieve this objective.

References

7 characteristics of DAO. (2019, November 2). Retrieved from Mercury.cash website: https://blog.mercury.cash/2019/11/02/7-characteristics-of-dao/

Web 1.0, Web 2.0, and Web 3.0 with their difference - GeeksforGeeks. (2018, September 24). Retrieved from Geeksforgeeks.org website: https://www.geeksforgeeks.org/web-1-0-web-2-0-and-web-3-0-with-their-difference/

BlockChannel. (2016, March 21). What is A "DAO"? How do they benefit consumers? Retrieved from BlockChannel website: https://medium.com/blockchannel/what-is-a-dao-how-do-they-benefit-consumers-f7a0a862f3dc

Hackl, C. (2021, June 1). What are DAOs, and why you should pay attention. Forbes Magazine. Retrieved from https://www.forbes.com/sites/cathyhackl/2021/06/01/what-are-daos-and-why-you-should-pay-attention/

Binance Academy. (2020, April 6). Decentralized Autonomous Organizations (DAOs) explained. Retrieved from Binance.com website: https://academy.binance.com/en/articles/decentralized-autonomous-organizations-daos-explained

Sharma, T. K. (2017, September 30). What is decentralized autonomous organization (DAO) & how DAO works? Retrieved from Blockchain-council.org website: https://www.blockchain-council.org/blockchain/decentralized-autonomous-organization-dao-dao-works/

Hackl, C. (2021, June 1). What are DAOs, and why you should pay attention. Forbes Magazine. Retrieved from https://www.forbes.com/sites/cathyhackl/2021/06/01/what-are-daos-and-why-you-should-pay-attention/

Hamacher, A. (2021, July 5). America's first legal DAO approved in Wyoming. Retrieved from Decrypt website: https://decrypt.co/75222/americas-first-dao-approved-in-wyoming

Kaal, W. A. (2020). Decentralized autonomous organizations – internal governance and external legal design. SSRN Electronic Journal. doi:10.2139/ssrn.3652481

(N.d.). Retrieved from Linkedin.com website: https://www.linkedin.com/pulse/why-dao-governance-matters-defi-dr-jane-thomason

Blockobi. (n.d.). Decentralized Organizations or DAO: The pros and cons – Blockobi Blog. Retrieved from Blockobi.com website: https://blockobi.com/blog/decentralized-organizations-or-dao-the-pros-and-cons/

Falkon, S. (2017, December 24). The story of the DAO — its history and consequences. Retrieved from The Startup website: https://medium.com/swlh/the-story-of-the-dao-its-history-and-consequences-71e6a8a551ee

Kaal, W. (2020, July 17). DAO Limitations - Wulf Kaal - Medium. Retrieved from Medium website: https://wulfkaal.medium.com/dao-limitations-a04526c936b

The advantages and disadvantages of A Dao. (2018, November 19). Retrieved from Cryptoswede.com website: https://www.cryptoswede.com/the-advantages-and-disadvantages-of-a-dao/

Bannon, S. (2016, May 16). The Tao of "The DAO" or: How the autonomous corporation is already here. TechCrunch. Retrieved from http://techcrunch.com/2016/05/16/the-tao-of-the-dao-or-how-the-autonomous-corporation-is-already-here/

(N.d.). Retrieved from Linkedin.com website: https://www.linkedin.com/pulse/decentralized-autonomous-organization-future-corporations-michiel-kok/

Mining, G. (2020, December 7). Everything you need to know about decentralized autonomous organizations (DAOs) — the DeFi series. Retrieved from Medium website: https://genesismining.medium.com/everything-you-need-to-know-about-decentralized-autonomous-organizations-daos-the-defi-series-b356d50467b8

(N.d.). Retrieved from Linkedin.com website: https://www.linkedin.com/pulse/why-dao-governance-matters-defi-dr-jane-thomason

UseTheBitcoin. (2018, August 22). Top five DAOs changing decentralization forever. Retrieved from Usethebitcoin.com website: https://usethebitcoin.com/top-five-daos-changing-decentralization-forever/

Bhalla, A. (2021, June 24). Top Decentralized Autonomous Organization (DAO) Projects to watch. Retrieved from Blockchain-council.org website: https://www.blockchain-council.org/blockchain/top-decentralized-autonomous-organization-dao-projects-to-watch/

Schout, G. (2020, May 1). The future of decentralization — DAOs - stakin - medium. Retrieved from Stakin website: https://medium.com/stakin/the-future-of-decentralization-daos-d8dc612f8be7

(N.d.). Retrieved from Computer.org website: https://www.computer.org/csdl/journal/oj/5555/01/09403889/1sLH87EtDK8

Dao, M. (2020, July 9). Why DAO's are the Future of Organisations? Retrieved from MANTRA DAO website: https://medium.com/mantra-dao/why-are-daos-the-future-of-organisations-cb46887c2446

The future is DAO: A primer on DAOs and their explosive growth. (2021, May 5). Retrieved from Underscore.vc website: https://underscore.vc/blog/the-future-is-dao-a-primer-on-daos-and-their-explosive-growth

Printed in Great Britain
by Amazon